ARO
NAILSEA
LONG ASHTON
AND
YATTON
IN OLD PHOTOGRAPHS

WRINGTON CHURCH AND THE DRING WAY, 1925. A small chained library still exists in the north aisle of the church.

THE ORIGINAL LORD NELSON INN BUILDING AT CLEEVE c. 1935, just prior to demolition. This was an old coaching inn, formerly called The Nelson Inn, with a shoeing smithy beside it. (See also page 139.)

AROUND
NAILSEA
LONG ASHTON
AND
YATTON
IN OLD PHOTOGRAPHS

COLLECTED BY

MICHAEL J. TOZER

ALAN SUTTON
1989

Alan Sutton Publishing
Gloucester

First published 1989

British Library Cataloguing in Publication Data

Around Nailsea, Long Ashton and Yatton in old photographs.
1. Avon. Nailsea district, history
I. Tozer, Michael
942.3'96

ISBN 0-86299-497-7

Typesetting and origination by
Alan Sutton Publishing
Printed in Great Britain by
WBC Print Ltd · Bristol

CONTENTS

THRESHING AT MR FRANK LUFF'S CHERRY TREE FARM, Kingston Seymour, in the First World War.

LONG ASHTON POST OFFICE c. 1913. Miss Emily Nurse, sub-postmistress here from before the First World War to the mid-1930s, stands in the doorway and her sister stands in the road with her bicycle.

INTRODUCTION

Little did I imagine as a schoolboy, commuting daily from Clevedon to Bristol nearly 50 years ago, that one day I would compile a book of photographs covering the area through which I was travelling.

My memories of the villages and countryside, through which I passed so regularly on the upper deck of a bus, are as clear as if I had made the journey only yesterday. At that time some of the scenes had changed little from the even earlier days that are recorded in the photographs in this book and, of these, some have altered very little to this day. Other remembered views have now disappeared completely but in most cases photographs have survived as a reminder of what was there. However, there were some temporary structures of which I have yet to find photographs.

One such example was the American Army's Second World War hospital camp in the grounds of Tyntesfield. As I remember it, this was an extensive collection of mainly brick-built single-storey buildings that covered a sizeable area of the parkland bordering the road between Wraxall village and the bottom of Belmont Hill. A recently acquired map of the area at that time has confirmed the position and layout of the buildings of this camp but, to date, I have not found any photographs of it. Wartime restrictions on photographing military installations may mean that a pictorial record of this camp has not survived, though it remained there for some years after the war, used for temporary housing accommodation during the time of acute shortage in Bristol, and its comparatively short-lived existence may be preserved only in the memories of those who saw it.

The inclusion of photographs from the 1860s in this book is due mainly to the survival of the albums of the prolific amateur photographer William Ravenhill Stock. W.R. Stock, born in Bristol on 21 October 1837, was a sugar importer and refiner. Following his marriage in February 1863 he lived first at Ashton Cottage, Long Ashton (later Ashover, next to the Congregational Church) and then, after suffering a severe financial loss when a ship load of sugar capsized and sank, bankrupting him, he was forced to sell this home, moving into Chelvey Rectory in July 1883. However, having finally won a long legal battle over the lost sugar he re-established his fortunes and built a house at Clevedon, which he called Chelvey House. He remained at Clevedon until his death in 1907, having moved to another house there in 1897 on his second marriage.

William Stock took a very active part in the public life of the day, was a regular correspondent to local newspapers and a close friend of many notable families in Bristol and Clevedon. His photography was of such quality that examples of his work appeared in national magazines. Many of his photographs of buildings were enhanced by the inclusion of a figure, often his wife, discreetly positioned in the foreground, as can be seen in the picture below.

Another photographer, many of whose pictures of the Nailsea and Wraxall areas appear in this book, was the Bristol professional John W. Garratt who, between around 1906 and 1935, published some 2,000 photographic views as picture postcards recording street scenes, events and buildings in Bristol and the surrounding villages. Individually printed, some of these photographs sold in considerable quantities. Most of these postcard photographs were taken between 1906 and 1914, and in the early 1920s, and his speciality was to include groups of children and/or contemporary road transport in his pictures.

A TYPICAL VICTORIAN PHOTOGRAPH taken by W.R. Stock at Cleeve in 1869.

This book, one of a series by Alan Sutton Publishing, covers that area in the north-west of the original county of Somerset between the areas covered in the publisher's companion volumes, *Around the Gordano Valley* and *Around Weston-super-Mare*, with the exception of the town of Clevedon which is to be covered in a forthcoming volume.

I have arranged the order of the photographs as a journey from the outskirts of Bristol to Tickenham and Nailsea, across the moors to Yatton and then from the Weston-super-Mare boundary along and around the A370 road to re-join the outward journey at Flax Bourton. I have used the captions to provide details which are not obvious from the photographs but are nevertheless relevant and, I hope, interesting additions to the visible record. Within the limited space available, many facts had to be omitted but some general information is included here as it is not specifically related to any photograph.

This was an area of early habitation, not just back to Roman days (building remains of which have been found at Long Ashton and Wraxall) but much earlier. Near Birdcombe Court a Stone-Age dwelling site has been found, one of very few known in the whole country, inhabited when this district resembled the arctic tundra. An Iron-Age torque (neck ornament) was also found nearby.

The industrial aspect of Nailsea is mentioned in the captions to the photographs of the Glassworks and coal mining relics. The considerable significance of the village in those days is supported by the intention in the early 1800s to construct a branch to serve the Nailsea industries from the proposed canal from Taunton to the River Avon at Pill. The canal (the only part completed was between Taunton and Bridgwater) would have generally followed the line of the M5 Motorway and the branch to Nailsea would have crossed Nailsea Moor and run parallel to the south sides of Silver Street and High Street terminating at the Glassworks, with a further short spur from it beside Station Road to Nailsea Coal Works. The canal company actually purchased land in Nailsea and this is why the 'Green' at the top of Station Road was still in private ownership in the 1940s. Glass, which had to be carefully packed, was difficult and coal expensive to transport over the poor roads of that time and the canal would have been an ideal answer. Later, glass was taken by road only as far as Bristol to continue its journey by rail or sea (glass was not despatched from Nailsea station until 1868, 27 years after its opening).

Approximate dates are given for photographs which cannot be dated exactly. Even where precise dates are quoted for an event or a building's construction, previously published references are often inconsistent and I have tried to check these against other sources to arrive at a correct date but, in some cases, I have had to make a reasonable deduction from the many alternatives available.

I hope the reader will find the photographs interesting and the captions informative, perhaps using the book as a guide to explore the area and compare scenes then and now. I certainly found it very enjoyable travelling around tracing the locations of many of these photographs.

Michael J. Tozer
1989

PUXTON STATION c. 1908. Loading churns of milk for delivery to Bristol. A group of churns on the opposite platform awaits collection by the next train to Weston-super-Mare.

The British Borderlands

THE SMYTH ARMS PUBLIC HOUSE at Ashton in 1867. Originally named The Coach and Horses, and dating from before 1578, the name was changed in 1860 to commemorate the family name of the owners of adjoining Ashton Court.

ASHTON GATE TOLLHOUSE, c. 1910. The turnpike road from Bristol to Hort's Batch in the Parish of Yatton started from here. The Ashton Gate Brewery buildings are on the right.

ASHTON GATE BREWERY TUG-OF-WAR TEAM, 1906. This brewery was taken over by Georges Brewery, Bristol (now part of the Courage Group) in 1932.

THE BRIDGE OVER THE RAILWAY at Ashton Gate in the 1930s. As motor traffic increased, this became a bottleneck with trams waiting at their terminus on the bridge. The line was, therefore, cut back to end in Ashton Road, just behind the camera.

ASHTON GATE STATION, on the line to Portishead, c. 1926. A simple wooden station opened at this site on 15 September 1906, to cater primarily for supporters attending the Bristol City F.C. ground after the club's promotion to the First Division in that year. Passenger numbers fell following the City's relegation in 1911, and the station closed in 1917. It was later rebuilt as seen here and re-opened on 22 May 1926. Closed on 7 September 1964, the station was again re-opened to handle only football 'specials' from 1970 to 1977 and yet again, for one week in May 1984 in connection with Billy Graham's Mission England meetings held at the City Ground. The track and platforms still survive.

IN THE AVON GORGE AT BOWER ASHTON. These two photographs, taken from the same position, show the changes necessary at this point to construct the Bristol to Portishead railway line. The photograph above, taken in May 1864, shows one of the tea-rooms (formerly known as Chocolate Houses) that were then popular summer rendezvous for Bristolians. The photograph below, taken in 1865, shows the aftermath of demolitions and the rock face being cut back preparatory to tunnelling through the rock projection in the centre of the view, directly below the Leigh tower of the Clifton Suspension Bridge.

CLIFTON BRIDGE STATION, 1867, looking towards Bristol. The station had been so recently completed that the contractor's materials are still lying in heaps on the river bank.

CLIFTON BRIDGE STATION, c. 1907, looking towards Portishead. Following closure on 7 September 1964, the station buildings were demolished and the site (with the exception of the platforms, footbridge and screen wall at the back of the 'up' platform which still survive) was used to erect the stables, kennels and administrative headquarters of the Avon and Somerset Constabulary's Mounted and Dog Section.

ASHTON MEADOWS, c. 1906. A column of people walking from Clifton Bridge station, on the left, towards Rownham Ferry to cross the river to Bristol.

ROWNHAM FERRY, c. 1900, looking from the Bristol bank towards Ashton Meadows. This ferry, formerly in a position lower down the river and originally owned by the Abbot of St Augustine's in Bristol, had been used by the monks to reach their retreat at Abbots Leigh.

ROWNHAM FERRY, c. 1904, looking down river with the Clifton Suspension Bridge in the background. The New Inn on the Somerset bank can be seen on the left. Intending passengers await the next boat. Accidents on the ferry were not uncommon, particularly when it was in its original position. Sir John Snygge drowned there on the night of 27 December 1610 as he was returning from Ashton Court and his body was not recovered until June 1611.

ROWNHAM FERRY, c. 1906. At low tide the ferry became just a bridge of boats for those brave enough to slide down and scramble up the muddy slipways. The ferry closed in 1932.

COMPARATIVE VIEWS FROM ROWNHAM HILL. Above, c. 1890, the New Inn in the foreground. Below, c. 1920, Swing Bridge and bonded warehouses erected and the former New Inn used as a laundry. The structures on the river bank at the top right in the upper photograph are shutes used to load coal, brought from the Ashton Vale collieries by tramway, into ships.

FROM ROWNHAM HILL, C. 1939. The same view as on page 18 but the New Inn building has been demolished and cleared away. Today this view is partially obscured by a new high level road crossing the river in the foreground.

GREVILLE SMYTH PARK, a popular area for relaxation, c. 1908. This park lies behind the trees in the upper right-hand corners of the preceding three photographs.

BRISTOL'S LADY MAYORESS, Mrs A.J. Smith, being taken across in her carriage after officially opening the Ashton Swing Bridge on 4 October 1906.

CROWDS WALKING ACROSS THE ASHTON SWING BRIDGE immediately after its opening on 4 October 1906.

ASHTON AVENUE C. 1907. Looking along the newly constructed road linking Ashton Gate to the Swing Bridge. Wide for its day, this road has since been further widened into a six-lane dual carriageway connecting with the new high level road complex over the river in the background. Greville Smyth Park lies beside this road, on the right.

A FOWLER TRACTION ENGINE-DRAWN FURNITURE WAGON TRAIN from Weston-super-Mare pauses outside the Smyth Arms, Ashton, c. 1905, to allow the crew to take refreshment before continuing their journey into Bristol. The crew have probably been on the road for four or five hours already and a mid-day break here would have been very welcome. As well as providing a source of creature comforts for the crew, a stop at such a location would also provide a ready supply of water to replenish the engine's tank far more easily than pumping it out of a roadside stream. These steam road locomotives, of which the Lalonde company had several, did not carry much water and replenishment stops had to be frequent. Lalonde's engines were a regular sight hauling loads over the roads of north Somerset until the arrival of the more versatile motor lorry but, even then, they were still invaluable for heavier loads over inferior roads.

LANE AT BOWER ASHTON is the title on the original, c. 1900, photograph. It is probably in the area around what is now Parklands Road. The wall on the left is of the pattern of the originally 12 ft high, approximately six-mile long wall with copper slag capping, built in the early 1800s to surround the Ashton Court Estate.

THE BRISTOL INTERNATIONAL EXHIBITION SITE at Ashton Meadows, viewed across the industrial buildings at Ashton Gate. The exhibition opened on 29 June 1914 but came to a premature end on 15 August when it was taken over by the War Office for use as army barracks. The railway line from Bristol to Ashton Gate snakes its way across the foreground.

THE FIGURE EIGHT COASTER scenic railway at the International Exhibition site in June 1914, just prior to its opening.

THE DOMINIONS PAVILION BUILDING AND BANDSTAND at the International Exhibition. The upper photograph, taken during construction, and the lower photograph, taken after completion, show the considerable size of the buildings erected for this exhibition. Even so, this was a small building compared with the International Pavilion which towered over the site and is seen at the left in the upper photograph on page 24. The Dominions Pavilion became the quarters of the 1st and 2nd Company of the Bristol Battalion, Gloucestershire Regiment following takeover by the War Office.

EXTERNAL AND INTERNAL VIEWS OF 'BRISTOL CASTLE' at the International Exhibition. Designed to represent what it was thought Bristol Castle (which had been demolished in 1655) may have looked like, the interior of this building was utilized to house a display of Bristol's history.

A GROUP OF CONSTRUCTION WORKERS pose in front of 'Bristol Castle' having completed their task.

ANOTHER PART OF THE INTERNATIONAL EXHIBITION SITE during construction, showing the replica of Drake's flagship *Revenge*, which had been built on dry land. In the background, the buildings of Clifton Bridge station stand above the exhibition backdrop fence.

MEMBERS OF THE PUBLIC in their summer finery enjoy the exhibition. The buildings in the background were mostly just shallow façades to give a backdrop to this side of the site but shops were built behind at ground floor level only.

'SHAKESPEARE'S ENGLAND' was the title given to this group of timber-framed buildings on the exhibition site.

MOVING BEDDING INTO THE DOMINIONS PAVILION, August 1914, preparatory to its occupation by the army.

BRISTOL CITY FOOTBALL CLUB'S GROUND, Ashton Gate. The scene on 24 May 1912 when 2,500 schoolchildren, appropriately dressed, formed a living Union Flag to celebrate Empire Day.

MADAM (LATER DAME) CLARA BUTT leaving the stand at Bristol City Football Club's ground, Ashton Gate, after watching the Empire Day celebrations, 24 May 1911.

A DEMONSTRATION OF MODERN METHODS OF PHYSICAL EDUCATION by 8,500 Bristol schoolchildren before Eustace Percy, President of the Board of Education, and 30,000 spectators at Bristol City Football Club's ground on 20 May 1926. This is part of a word tableau reading 'PHYSICAL TRAINING DEMONSTRATION, BRISTOL – SCHOOLS.'

AN EARLY MOTOR CHARABANC of the Bristol Tramways and Carriage Company is posed in 1911 for an official photograph on the road outside Grass Lodge (also known as Town Lodge), the Ashton Court Estate gateway which is just beyond Ashton Gate on the A370 road to Weston-super-Mare. The vehicle, which was constructed entirely in the BT & CC's own workshops, was first licensed for use on 1 June 1911 and was designed to be a considerable improvement on the charabancs then currently operating. It was provided with a fixed wooden roof and side curtains for the protection of passengers in inclement weather; a far superior arrangement to the normal canvas cover which had to be erected and then taken down every time a storm was encountered.

A LOGGING TEAM, heading for Bristol, passes Ashton Court's Grass Lodge, c. 1910.

THE WEST FRONT, ASHTON COURT with grazing deer, c. 1905. This photograph, possibly taken by Gilbert Irby the husband of the last of the Smyths of Ashton Court, the Hon. Esmé (or even by Esmé herself as both were keen photographers) was used by Esmé as a postcard to send to a friend on 14 September 1905. It has been claimed that Ashton Court grounds contain the oldest continuously inhabited deer park in the country, the park having been enclosed in 1392. The Smyths had been owners since 1545.

THE SOUTH FRONT, ASHTON COURT, c. 1910. The left-hand section dates from c. 1635, the right-hand from c. 1810 and the central clock tower is an early nineteenth-century reconstruction of a c. 1550 gatehouse. The core of the building dates from c. 1390 with additions during and shortly after the Elizabethan period.

THE LONG ASHTON TO BRISTOL HORSE-DRAWN BUS stops outside the Smyth Arms, c. 1885. Comparing this photograph with the earlier one on page 11 shows that the Georgian first floor windows had by now been replaced with plain sashes.

A CLASSICAL DANCING DISPLAY at a fête in aid of the Seamen's and Boatmen's Friendly Society, held at Ashton Court on 12 July 1930. Left to right: Majorie Clark, Dorothy Davis, Patti Jones and Dorothy Oram.

By the High Road to Tickenham

THE FAILAND INN, FAILAND, c. 1906. Built c. 1860 to replace the original inn of the same name, it stands beside the coach road from Clevedon to Bristol. This road had been realigned following the enclosure of open land in the first half of the nineteenth century leaving the original hostelry (later to become part of Failand Lodge Farm) some way off the main road.

CHURCH LODGE, c. 1906, the last of the Ashton Court Lodge Gates to be built, late in the nineteenth century. Situated at the bottom of the hill through Clarken Combe to Failand, this lodge replaced a simple iron gate in the boundary wall of the Smyth's estate.

CLARKEN COMBE LODGE, c. 1905. A much more impressive structure, built in the early nineteenth century, halfway up Clarken Combe. The lodge cannot be seen so clearly today as trees and other vegetation have grown up in front of it.

TYNTESFIELD, the home of Lord Wraxall, c. 1912. The name Tyntesfield derives from the Tynte family who held this land at Wraxall in the fourteenth century. This fine house is set deep within its park so cannot be seen clearly from surrounding roads.

TYNTESFIELD, c. 1920. The visible parts of the house date from 1862–64 and surround an original building of c. 1820.

TYNTESFIELD, 1867, showing the large conservatory then recently completed, which has since been demolished.

TYNTESFIELD, c. 1912. The main entrance with its ornate tower is on the left and the chapel, built between 1872–75, later than the main building, is on the right.

WRAXALL, C. 1912. The Battle Axes Hotel, on the left, has had many titles. The 1837 Tithe map shows it as Gordon's Crest Inn. Directories from 1861 to 1882 list it as Wraxall Inn. The Ordnance Survey map of 1884 shows it as Chequers Inn. From c. 1889 it was the Battle Axes (from the coat of arms of the Gibbs family of Tyntesfield who owned it) until sold by this family without the right to the use of the name. It was then renamed the Widdecombe Arms but now carries its sixth name as the New Battle Axes Hotel.

THE ORIGINAL WRAXALL VILLAGE CLUB, C.1904, attached to, but not part of the Battle Axes Hotel. This building was also owned by the Tyntesfield Estate but, following a disagreement with Lord Wraxall, the members left here and moved to a new club building further along the road. It is now part of the hotel.

A GROUP OF CYCLISTS heads away from the Battle Axes Hotel towards Wraxall Church, c. 1908. The post office, on the right, closed some time ago and the building is now used by a hairdresser. The 'WRAXALL' name-plate seen at the top right survives, refixed in a lower position on the wall.

LOOKING TOWARDS WRAXALL CHURCH, C. 1908. The piles of stones lining the gutter, either intended for or the remains of road repairs, probably came from the adjacent quarry.

THE CROSS TREE, Wraxall, c. 1912. This elm had been planted in 1650 to replace a stone preaching cross destroyed by Cromwell's Roundheads in 1649. Surviving for 320 years, despite being twice struck by lightning, it finally succumbed to Dutch Elm disease and was felled in May 1977. A horse-chestnut was planted here in November 1977 to continue the Cross Tree tradition.

ALL SAINTS' CHURCH, Wraxall, behind the Cross Tree, c. 1908. The shape of the tree shows evidence of the damage caused by the lightning strikes.

WRAXALL CHURCHYARD, C. 1908. The detached building on the left was the original village school, built 1801 and containing timbers from a 'man-of-war' ship broken up at Bristol. This building was later used to house the church library when a new school was built in 1856. When a second school building was opened in 1881 for girls and infants the 1856 building became a school for boys only. This boys' school closed in the late 1930s and was later used as the Wraxall Social Centre but the girls' building, apparently with 1902 additions, is still in use.

JUBILEE COTTAGES, Wraxall, C. 1908. Almshouses for retired servants from Tyntesfield.

WRAXALL COURT, C. 1912. Built C. 1720 and incorporating the entrance porch from an earlier building of 1658, it was considerably enlarged in 1830. Marion Beloe was living here with her widowed mother at the time of her marriage to William Stock, several of whose photographs are reproduced in this book.

WRAXALL COTTAGE, C. 1905. Rather large for the title of 'cottage' (only half the length of the building is seen) this is an isolated house, extended from the original 'cottage' section on the Tyntesfield Estate in the hillside opposite the Battle Axes.

BIRDCOMBE COURT, Wraxall, c. 1912, also known as Tower House, is a remarkable survival of a thirteenth-century manor house. The tower, with its doorways of carriage-way width, originally stood separately in front of the house; the joining wings are later additions.

WRAXALL MILL, c. 1925. This mill ceased working around 1900 and, with the adjoining cottage/shop, was demolished for road re-alignment after the Second World War. The old road, with bridge wall beside the River Land Yeo, survives as a lay-by outside the entrance to the adjoining Wraxall House.

WRAXALL HOUSE, c. 1908. Built c. 1600 and extended later, it was a private residence with many successive owners until recent times. It was then used for various purposes, the last being as a privately-run residential home for the mentally handicapped. It was converted to a hotel in 1989. Inset into a garden wall in the grounds are the millstones from the adjoining Wraxall Mill.

EAST END, Nailsea, c. 1906. The scattered houses along the winding road from Wraxall to Nailsea with Wraxall Church tower just visible in the distance in the centre of the view.

NEW RANK, Nailsea, c. 1912. This rank of terraced houses, of which only the eastern end is in this view, was built opposite the glassworks in the 1820s to provide additional housing for the glassworkers. (Old Rank, or Whitcombe's Rank, on the opposite side of the road, part of which survives in Woodview Terrace, was the original glassworkers' housing.)

NAILSEA HIGH STREET, c. 1904. The building with the balcony, in the centre of this picture taken from the roof of the glassworks, was one of the first shops in the street, opened by 1844 and which has, so far, survived. The building immediately beyond was Mr Bowden's shop.

NAILSEA HIGH STREET, C. 1912. A bread delivery cart advertising 'Genuine Brown Bread' passes Charles Bowden's grocery and drapery premises which carry an eye-catching advertisement. The central building is part of the glassworks and the Royal Oak Hotel flies its flag high from a pole lashed to a tree in the forecourt.

NAILSEA HIGH STREET, C. 1912. A view in the opposite direction to the upper one on this page, towards the so-called 'village green'.

THE ROYAL OAK HOTEL, Nailsea, C. 1905. The figure in the doorway could be the proprietor, Stephen Ansell, who also ran a brewery, supplying his own and other public houses.

NAILSEA RIFLE CLUB'S RIFLE RANGE, C. 1910, in the long room next to the Royal Oak Hotel. This illustration is taken from a postcard which was printed for Mr Ansell to use in correspondence in connection with his hotel.

THE TOP END OF HIGH STREET, Nailsea, c. 1907, with 11 children and an adult carefully posed by the photographer. High Street had originally been known as Nailsea Heath Road and later as New Church Road.

MR FREDERICK SMALLMAN holds the reins of the donkey cart outside Elizabeth Waymouth's stationery shop in Nailsea High Street, c. 1890. Mr Smallman became a master decorator. In 1924 his wife opened a retail paint shop on the corner of Silver Street and Clevedon Road which became a builders' merchant/DIY complex c. 1955 and was demolished in 1971.

THE DEVELOPMENT OF NAILSEA'S SHOPPING AREA. The photographs on this page show the view from the post office looking down High Street in c. 1900 (above) with two glassworks cones still standing in the distance, and c. 1911 (below) when the cones had been demolished and the property on the corner of Clevedon Road had been built. The upper photograph on the next page shows a similar view in the 1930s after the shop rank (on the left) had been built in Silver Street. All the visible buildings on the left of these pictures were demolished in 1971 for the town centre redevelopment.

THIS C. 1905 VIEW IN THE OPPOSITE DIRECTION to the three preceding views shows the post office beyond the 'Green' and the Queen's Head, converted from a former private dwelling, on the corner of Station Road. The Queen's Head and part of the 'Green' survive. A plaque in the new shopping precinct records that the 'Green' was given to the Parish of Nailsea in 1948 by Miss Fanny E. Russell. Its shape was altered in 1974 to fit the new pedestrian area but brass studs were set into the paving to mark its original boundary.

NAILSEA POST OFFICE, housed in George Russell's drapery shop, c. 1912. The Russell family had owned the 'Green' in front of this block of buildings which was demolished in 1971.

THE BRISTOL TRAMWAYS AND CARRIAGE COMPANY'S BUS TERMINUS outside Nailsea Post Office, 1914. This motor bus service had been extended from its former terminus at Long Ashton on 24 October 1913 and was later further extended to Clevedon. Seven round trips per day were run on weekdays and Sundays with 11 trips on Saturdays – fare 8*d*. (3p) each way. The unqualified 'driver' at the wheel would not have been approved by the company.

CHILDREN OF THE PAROCHIAL (OLD CHURCH) SCHOOL, Nailsea, c. 1904. Two public elementary schools were operating in Nailsea at this date. The Parochial School was the older with accommodation for 210 children and Christ Church School, opened in 1844, had accommodation for 170 children. Both survive today but are now named Grove Junior School and Four Oaks Infants School respectively.

NAILSEA OLD BOYS FOOTBALL TEAM 1908/9 season.

SILVER STREET, Nailsea, c. 1912, looking towards Kingshill from the Christ Church end. The wind pump, just visible on the skyline above the group of children in the road, drew water from a deep well for use in Mr Henry Bougourd's market garden and greenhouses on the corner of Whitesfield Road (formerly Back Lane).

SILVER STREET, Nailsea, c. 1912. The house on the left, now No. 34a/34b Silver Street, was then called Moorfields Cottage. Moorfields House stands behind the trees in the centre of the view.

SILVER STREET, Nailsea, c. 1912, looking towards Christ Church. The building on the left is Church House, constructed in 1910. Silver Street is one of the older roads in Nailsea, in existence long before the present town centre was developed on the former Nailsea Heath.

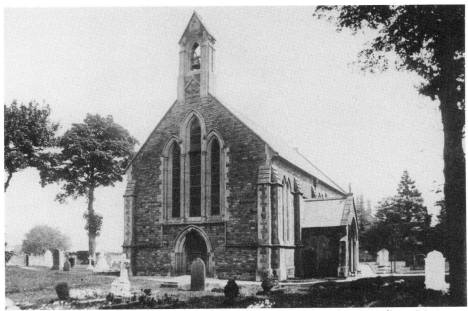

CHRIST CHURCH, Nailsea, c. 1912. Built in 1843 and then in quiet rural surroundings, it is now a peaceful 'pocket' on the edge of the town's recently developed shopping area.

STATION ROAD, Nailsea, c. 1912. A view along the road (formerly called Goddins Lane and Bullocks Lane) looking in the direction of today's new shopping precinct.

ASH HAYES LANE junction with Station Road. c. 1912. An area of much house building during the earlier years of this century.

GEORGE ('TURFY') RENDELL, horse dealer and butcher, with his cart outside his house in Silver Street, c. 1913.

NAILSEA FIRE BRIGADE, c. 1907, posed in front of a number of posters advertising the visit of Hanneford's Circus and Menagerie.

THE ORIGINAL MEDIEVAL CENTRE OF NAILSEA around the fourteenth-century Holy Trinity Church, c. 1910. Now it is surrounded by modern housing developments.

COTTAGES IN OLD CHURCH ROAD, c. 1912. Despite the large scale house building that has since taken place around the area, this view is almost unchanged. Old Church Road is now blocked off just behind the camera position and its former line across the fields to join Station Road is now made up of Haslands, Beckets Lane, Little Meadow End and Farlers End.

HOLY TRINITY CHURCH, Nailsea, c. 1910. The building on the far right was the Parish Room where the Vestry met. The Vestry comprised the Churchwardens, the Overseers of the Poor, the Surveyor of the Highways, the Constable and the Haywarden. The War Memorial was erected in the centre of the view after the First World War and the Parish Room was demolished in 1963.

KINGSHILL FARM, c. 1910. The main farmhouse, one of many similar that encircled Nailsea, survives today but the thatched roof has been replaced by tiles. When this work was being carried out a receipt was found recording payments for the billeting of Roundhead troops in March 1643.

BUCKLANDS BATCH, C. 1900. On the road from Nailsea looking towards Backwell, this rural area saw considerable housing development from the turn of this century and was soon linked to the older areas of Nailsea. This section of quiet lane, hardly altered, is now part of this major road between Nailsea and Backwell.

THE ENGINE HOUSE AND CHIMNEY OF FARLERS PIT, Nailsea, c. 1912, seen from the junction of Old Church Road (left) and Station Road (right). Farlers coal mine, one of many in the Nailsea area, opened in 1848 but ceased working in 1860 due to flooding. The Engine House, however, still survives adjoining Queens Road which replaced Old Church Road here on a slightly different alignment. The signpost survives in its original position and so, today, marks where Old Church Road formerly joined Station Road.

NAILSEA AND BACKWELL STATION, C. 1912. Opened on 14 June 1841 as Nailsea station on the Bristol and Exeter Railway, it was given its later name on 1 May 1905. Although closed to goods traffic on 1 July 1964, the station remains open to passengers but the handsome buildings in this photograph have been replaced with ugly bus-type platform shelters.

THE VIEW FROM NAILSEA STATION, looking towards Bucklands Batch, Nailsea, C. 1905.

A PANORAMIC VIEW OF NAILSEA GLASSWORKS from Scotch Horn, c. 1900, (above) and a view of the ruins, c. 1908, (below). John Robert Lucas ran a beer and cider works in Bristol and had shares in a glass bottle works there and in another at Stanton Wick. In 1788 he decided to start his own glassworks and chose a six-acre site called Cooles Close on Nailsea Heath to build a works which would concentrate on the production of crown window glass and bottles. The works eventually covered a 13-acre area on the south side of what is now High Street from the Royal Oak to Nailsea Park and prospered due to the ready local availability of stone for building, lime and sand for the glass and coal for firing the kilns. As late as 1819, when glassmaking was declining rapidly in Bristol, Lucas built a new cone (on the left in the view above).

EXTERNAL AND INTERNAL VIEWS OF THE GLASSWORKS RUINS, c. 1908. Following the death of Lucas in 1828 the works continued in production under other owners, the last being Chance Bros., a firm founded by Lucas' nephew, but by then bottlemaking had ceased and the Nailsea works produced only sheet window glass. The end came, however, in 1873 when the local coal supply ran out. The plant and machinery were removed to Chance's works at Birmingham but attempts to sell the site for housing development were unsuccessful. A few of the buildings remain today – some of the Old Rank houses and the Manager's house in what is now Woodview Terrace, the office block on High Street and a gas-fired kiln building adjoining the Royal Oak, but most of the remainder of the site has remained derelict.

THE DEMOLITION OF THE NEW CONE at Nailsea Glassworks. The cone was blown up on 8 June 1905 with the intention of selling the bricks, but this venture was not particularly successful and eventually much of it was used as hardcore under the runway extension built at Filton, Bristol, in 1947 for the Brabazon aircraft trials.

THE ROAD FROM NAILSEA TO TICKENHAM, c. 1912. Known originally as Black Road and later as Clevedon Road this country lane, widened in part only and still bordered by some of the original trees, now carries somewhat more traffic than the occasional horse and cart.

Over
the Moors

THIS WOLSELEY CAR, new in 1914, with attendant chauffeurs, maids and other servants, is thought to be in the stable yard at Nailsea Court some time in the early 1920s.

KENN POST OFFICE, C. 1908. The village of Kenn, on the moor road from Clevedon to Yatton, is a very small hamlet. However, it has a claim to fame – the last public hanging in Somerset took place here behind the Drum and Monkey (formerly the Rose and Crown) in 1832.

SKATING ON KENN POND. A photograph taken by W.R. Stock in February 1895. This large pond had been used as a duck decoy from olden days and is clearly marked as such on eighteenth-century maps.

THE CHURCH OF ST JOHN THE EVANGELIST at Kenn, c. 1909. This scene has changed little in 80 years though the tree has lost a few more branches. The cottage was once an antiques shop.

BREWING TEA AT KENN, 1890. This is another W.R. Stock photograph. Although an amateur photographer, he was a master craftsman in this field and this photograph shows an apparently spontaneous, though actually deliberately posed, record of Victorian times in the lives of his more wealthy friends.

ANOTHER TEA DRINKING GROUP AT KENN by W.R. Stock, February 1895. A much more formal and obviously posed photograph.

KINGSTON SEYMOUR MANOR HOUSE. This ancient building, burnt down in the mid-nineteenth century, was home to the Seymour family which gave its name to the village to distinguish it from other 'Kingston' villages. One of the earlier Seymours was a Baron present at King John's signing of the Magna Carta.

KINGSTON SEYMOUR was an area liable to extensive flooding in earlier times. Banks were constructed to alleviate the problem and this group of horsemen is taking part in the ceremony of Riding the Banks in 1915. Known names among the group are: John, John Hugh and Tom Burdge, Ben Crossman, Charles and Edward Griffin, Frank Luff, Albert Masters, Robert Norton, Herbert Price, Walter and William Stuckey, Frank and Henry Sweet and William Travis.

THE VILLAGE GREEN, Kingston Seymour, c. 1922. Of the 11 then recently pollarded trees on the Green at this date, three survive today and some more recently planted saplings have replaced the other eight which had to be felled.

RUSTIC FARM, Kingston Seymour, c. 1914. William and Ellen Stuckey stand behind the gate and in front, left to right, are their children Percy, Frank, Arthur, Reginald, Lillian and Gertie.

A VIEW ACROSS THE CORNER OF THE GREEN at Kingston Seymour, c. 1921, to the post office located in what was then known locally as Triangle House. The post office has since closed and the building, now wholly residential, is named Benthams House. The War Memorial, centre, re-used the base from the old village cross which was lying discarded beneath these trees in 1877 according to a contemporary report.

THE REVD MAJOR REVEL RAYNER GREEN stands with the new treble bell, cast in 1930 to celebrate his appointment as Rector of All Saints' Church, Kingston Seymour. He had been Curate-in-charge of the church for the preceding 25 years. The addition of this bell to the church gave it a peal of six bells.

THE LYCH-GATE, All Saints' Church, Kingston Seymour, c. 1912. In the church is an inscribed board recording an inundation of sea water on 20 January 1606 when many persons and cattle were drowned and the water was five feet high in the building.

EDWARD GRIFFIN of Rookery Farm, Kingston Seymour, completing a 50-year unbroken record of mowing the same hayfield, having started soon after the turn of this century.

MIDDLE FARM, Kingston Seymour, c. 1900. William and Anne Marie Gage with their sons George, Charles and William Henry.

THE HARVEST HOME COMMITTEE, Kingston Seymour, c. 1900. The Revd George Herbert Smyth-Pigott with John Fowles, two members of the Gage family (probably George and William), Alfred, Edward and Sidney Griffin, Tom Jones, Mr Naish, Thomas Phippen, James Smith, William and Henry(?) Stuckey, Philip(?) Wilcox, Albert and William(?) Williams. Sidney Griffin was a grocer and the local sub-postmaster, James Smith was the school-master and many of the others were local farmers.

A TRAIN LEAVES KINGSTON ROAD STATION, Kingston Seymour, for Clevedon on the independent Weston, Clevedon and Portishead Light Railway line, 1935. Kingston Seymour had no less than four stations, if such a grand term can be applied to what were basically milk churn platforms with adjacent huts for any intending passengers to wait in, at Mud Lane, Ham Lane, Broadstone (opened 1918 for passengers only) and Kingston Road (the milk platform was removed in the early 1930s). This section of the line had opened on 1 December 1897 and was closed on 18 May 1940.

ST MARY'S CHURCH AND THE RECTORY, Yatton, from the National School, c. 1900. A group of men are loading horse-drawn carts on The Waste. The walled area on the left is now a car park and The Waste has been neatly grassed over but otherwise the area is much the same today. The small building on the right was the village lock-up.

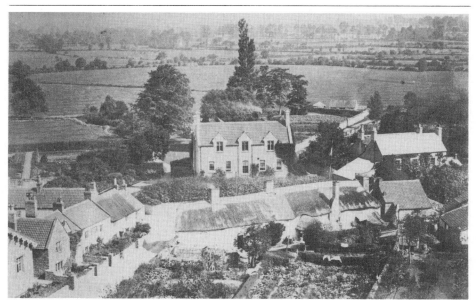

VIEWS FROM YATTON CHURCH TOWER. Above, C. 1870, looking towards the Vicarage. Church Road on the left and Grey House on the right survive virtually unchanged but all of the other buildings have since been demolished. Most of the rank of old cottages bordering High Street, centre foreground, had gone by 1885 and the cottage, extreme right, by 1921 but the house on the corner of the Causeway survived until the 1950s. The garden area in the foreground became the school's playground and is now a car park. Below, C. 1905, a group of children outside the school look at a car parked on the edge of The Waste, exactly where the church car park is today.

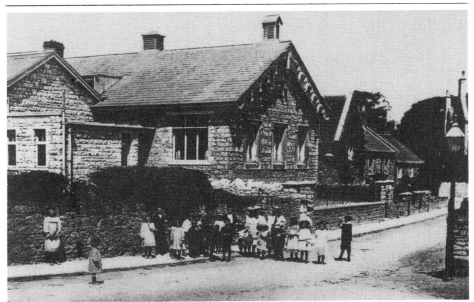

THE NATIONAL SCHOOL, Church Road, Yatton, c. 1909. Built in 1834 for 164 children and enlarged in 1904 to accommodate 228 pupils, the school closed some time ago and is now being converted for other uses.

LOOKING ALONG CHURCH ROAD towards the Vicarage, c. 1935. The gate pillars in the wall on the right framed the entrance to the school's playground (now a car park). The Vicarage has been demolished and new housing erected on the site. A replacement Vicarage stands on the opposite side of Well Lane.

HIGH STREET, Yatton, then called Station Road, c. 1905. On the left of this muddy winter scene is the entrance to The Avenue and the second building was then the post office. The early motor car on the right carries the registration BF 15, a rare 1903 number issued in Staffordshire. The letters BF were not continued due to their connection with the initials of a derogatory expression.

CARTS PARKED OUTSIDE YATTON POST OFFICE, c. 1908. With a rebuilt frontage, this survived as the post office until replaced by the present building opposite the new shopping precinct. A link with the past continues, however, as outside the new post office the letter box on the forecourt is a rare survivor, outside London, of only 75 boxes of an experimental type with built-in stamp machines manufactured in 1932.

HIGH STREET, Yatton, c. 1908, when the road was much narrower at this point than it is today and large trees were still standing in adjacent gardens.

HIGH STREET, Yatton, c. 1908. The road here was then adequate for the passage of horse-drawn carts but, with the coming of the motor age, was widened following tree felling and removal of the end of the projecting wing on the Prince of Orange.

MRS ANN PEARCE outside her shop in High Street, Yatton, c. 1930. Mrs Pearce traded here from c. 1920 to the late 1930s, but the lorry at the back of the yard, apparently having had some years' use, had not been registered until early 1925.

A PANORAMIC VIEW OF YATTON STATION, c. 1905. The station opened on 14 June 1841, with the name Clevedon Road, on the newly constructed Bristol and Exeter Railway. It was renamed Yatton on 28 July 1847 when the branch line to Clevedon was opened. This view of the south end of the station in its heyday shows, from left to right: a train waiting to leave for Clevedon; the rear end of a train from Weston-super-Mare heading towards Bristol; a train from London, via Bristol, about to depart for Weston-super-Mare and south-west England; a train ready to leave on either the branch line to Cheddar and Wells (opened 3 August 1869) or to Wrington and Blagdon (opened 4 December 1901); spare carriage stock and the Goods Shed. The part of the branch line to Blagdon beyond Congresbury closed to passengers on 14 September 1931 and the section beyond Wrington closed to goods traffic on 1 November 1950, though goods were still carried as far as Wrington until 8 June 1963. The whole branch from Yatton to Wells was closed to passengers on 9 September 1963 and to goods traffic on 1 July 1964. Goods traffic ceased totally at Yatton on 29 November 1965 and the last passenger service on the branch to Clevedon ran on 3 October 1966. This chronology records the gradual rise and then sharp decline in importance of Yatton station but today, refurbished, it sees many local and inter-city trains on the line to and from Bristol and the facility of a free car park for anyone travelling by rail is an incentive to its use.

THE CLEVEDON BRANCH TRAIN waits in its bay platform at Yatton while a diesel railcar on a local Weston-super-Mare to Bristol run stops at the main 'up' platform on the right.

STATION STAFF POSE ON YATTON STATION, 20 May 1892. The Railway Hotel, in the background, has now been renamed The Firebox.

AN ALMOST DESERTED HIGH STREET, Yatton, with very rough edges to the road, c. 1906.

STATION ROAD, Yatton (now part of High Street), near the railway station, c. 1908.

LOOKING FROM THE TOP OF THE STATION APPROACH ROAD, Yatton, towards Clevedon, along what was then known as Hill View, c. 1912. Albert Ernest Bird's Albert Mews, now a kitchen and bedroom furniture establishment, advertised 'Good Stabling, Cabs to Meet All Trains, Wedding and Funeral Carriages, Pony Trap and Wagonette for Hire'. George Gage, next door, also advertised a pony carriage for hire and the availability of a cycle storage shed.

YATTON HIGH STREET, C. 1915, with carts parked in the forecourt of the Prince of Orange and posters encouraging men to enlist for service in the army in France. This long-established hostelry building is the result of extensions to an original c. 1650 two-room house.

LOOKING IN THE OPPOSITE DIRECTION to the upper photograph on this page. The sign just visible on the left was for William Tutt's grocery stores. Mr Tutt suggested that you should 'Stop Here for the Best of Everything'. The projecting wing of the Prince of Orange, in the centre of the picture, was later cut back for road widening.

ROBERT CHAMBERS' BAKER'S SHOP AND REFRESHMENT ROOMS, High Street, Yatton. The wedding cake in the window was for the wedding reception of his youngest daughter Rosina Mary who was married at St Mary's Church on 5 September 1904 to Harry Burgoyne of Plymouth.

ISAAC JOULES was a farmer's son who married a gipsy maid and was disowned by his family. After his wife Merrily's death in 1827 he frequently spent whole nights by her grave in Yatton churchyard until he died on 10 April 1841, aged 70, and was buried beside her.

CATTLE BEING DRIVEN ALONG THE ROAD at Horsecastle, Yatton, c. 1907.

COURT HOUSE FARM, Yatton, c. 1900. This old building survived in this form until the 1950s when the thatch was replaced by tiles. It was eventually demolished in the mid-1960s to make way for the new shopping precinct.

CHURCH CAUSEWAY, Yatton, c. 1910. The gate in the foreground survives, hung on new posts, but not the stile or the cottage which was demolished by 1921.

AN INTERESTED GROUP POSE FOR THE PHOTOGRAPHER to take this view of Claverham Road, c. 1920.

SIDNEY LAWRENCE ADVERTISES HIS TRADES as builder, carpenter and wheelwright on the front of this building in Claverham, c. 1906. Mr Lawrence was also the village sub-postmaster and the entrance to the post office is at the side in High Street. Today, the side entrance has been blocked up, the building raised to two storeys at the back and the whole ground floor frontage is the village shop and post office.

HIGH STREET, Claverham, in the late 1920s or 1930s. A view past the post office on the left, where the telephone has arrived to the United Methodist Chapel which had been built in 1867. The chapel has since been converted into a dwelling house.

AN EDWARDIAN SCENE, Claverham, c. 1908.

CHELVEY IS A TINY HAMLET, reputedly one of the smallest villages in England, where no modern development has taken place. The scene here, c. 1910, is probably almost the same as it was in medieval days and is certainly, apart from the horse and cart, how it looks today.

CHELVEY COURT, c. 1906. With the adjoining twelfth-century Church of St Bridget, rectory and ancient barn, this remaining part of the original Court, which had been erected in the thirteenth century, rebuilt in the early seventeenth century and converted to a farmhouse about 300 years ago, forms the centre of Chelvey. The grand entrance, an addition of c. 1620 to the original building and known as Solomon's Porch, can be seen on the left.

NAILSEA COURT, c. 1909. A near neighbour of Chelvey Court (with a shared swannery) and dating from c. 1250, the buildings seen today are mostly of the fifteenth and sixteenth centuries, the roof being raised at the end of the seventeenth century to give a three-storey building. The Court was used as a farmhouse for 160 years from 1745; its condition steadily declined and the south wing collapsed during this period. Lieutenant Commander Charles E. Evans bought it in 1906 and during the next seven years carried out extensive restoration and rebuilding. The photograph on the left shows the state of the building at the completion of the first phase of restoration with the first version of the tower in the centre.

NAILSEA COURT, c. 1912. The end of the second phase of restoration, showing the redesigned tower which then more successfully matched the rest of the building. Commander Evans had collected every bit of stone, wood and iron he could find from the original building, including those materials that had been taken from the south wing ruins to build barns and estate walls, and more materials of the same style from other sources, including a large quantity from Over Langford (or Upper Langford) Manor House.

NAILSEA COURT, c. 1920. With materials obtained from Langford, Commander Evans rebuilt the south wing, seen on the left, incorporating the second tower, to complete the restoration.

THE GREAT HALL, Nailsea Court, c. 1920, panelled throughout with oak from Langford.

NAILSEA COURT, c. 1920. In the dining room, above, the panelling, chimney-piece and unique 'Nailsea door', carved on both sides of its upper panel, are from the original building. The withdrawing room, below, has the original chimney-piece, which had stood in the open, covered with a vine, for more than a century; the stone, floor, panelling and plaster panel above the fireplace were from Langford and the ceiling was from Ashley Manor in Bristol.

Around the River Yeo

THE SHIP AND CASTLE, C. 1908. This old inn has stood behind Congresbury's ancient cross since at least the eighteenth century. Horse-drawn brakes travelling between Bristol and Weston-super-Mare changed horses here on the outward and return journeys.

ST. GEORGES, on the outskirts of Weston-super-Mare, in the 1950s. The name is now more familiar to motorists as the site of the M5 Motorway junction, but here a coach carrying Birmingham holidaymakers passes the Woolpack Inn, named after a wool packing station which once operated nearby, on the old A370 road.

THE THIRTEENTH-CENTURY CHURCH OF ST SAVIOUR, Puxton, c. 1930. The leaning tower is a noted external feature, but the interior is also interesting with its ancient seating, including box pews, as though time had stood still here for centuries.

PUXTON STATION, c. 1906, looking towards Worle. This station opened on 14 June 1841, with the name Banwell. Changed to Worle on 3 August 1869 and to Puxton on 1 March 1884 when a new station was opened at Worle, its final name change was on 1 March 1922 when it became Puxton and Worle, two months after the closure of Worle station. Goods traffic ceased on 10 June 1963 and the final closure of the station to passengers was on 6 April 1964.

STAFF POSE WITH THE MILK CHURNS on Puxton station, c. 1908.

HEWISH, C. 1906. A quiet country road but the motor age was not far away – an early car is parked behind the horse and cart. Behind the tree on the left is St Anne's Church, unusual in that it has no tower. A tower was intended but when building had reached a height of 70 ft the foundations gave way, the unfinished tower fell and was not rebuilt.

HEWISH IN THE 1920s. The motor age has arrived and the resulting road widening and realignment along the A370 from Bristol to Weston-super-Mare makes it difficult to realise that this photograph was taken from almost the same position less than 20 years after the upper one on this page, though it was still safe enough to stand in the road.

HEWISH IN THE 1930s. From the same position as the preceding photograph but ten years later, when electricity had arrived in the village and the motor car was king of the road.

HEWISH POST OFFICE AND STORES in the 1930s. Typical of a village store on a main road, the owner Mr E.L. Hobbs tried to attract as much trade as possible. As well as grocery, confectionery, drapery and hardware for the local village, he advertised his tea-gardens, home-grown fruit, home-made jams, even seeds for the garden, to attract potential customers as they passed in their cars. It was fortunate for Mr Hobbs that the road realignment had left a lay-by outside his shop for parking.

IN THE GRANGE, Hewish, 1910. Probably Mrs Harding, widow of Stephen Harding, a farmer who had lived here for many years.

THE CROSS ROADS, Congresbury, c. 1910, with a group of cyclists taking a rest beside the village cross outside the Ship and Castle.

THE OLD BRIDGE OVER THE RIVER YEO at Congresbury, carrying the road from Bristol past the side of the Ship and Castle, c. 1906. Broad Street is ahead and the road to Weston-super-Mare leads off to the right past the signpost.

CONGRESBURY'S VILLAGE CROSS and Station Road in the 1930s. This well preserved fifteenth-century cross is actually taller than it appears as two more steps of the base were buried when the surrounding road level was raised.

THE WEIR ON THE RIVER YEO at Congresbury, c. 1904. Although far inland, it is to this point on the river that normal tides flow and the former West Mill stood here.

BOATING ON THE RIVER at Congresbury, c. 1920. The Yeo river here was a popular venue for fishing enthusiasts from Bristol. They would leave their rods hanging from the ceiling of The Plough Inn from one weekend to the next.

BRINSEA ROAD, Congresbury, c. 1904. On the right is Yeo Meads, on the left Fernbank and, beyond it, the Methodist Chapel.

THE POST OFFICE, Station Road, Congresbury, c. 1910, when John Pitts was sub-postmaster, before Mrs Adelaide Kitchen became sub-postmistress. Both Mr Pitts and Mrs Kitchen published a range of picture postcards of Congresbury so recording for future generations the appearance of the village from 1900 to 1930.

THE METHODIST CHAPEL, Congresbury, erected in 1878 at a cost of £620, with the obligatory group posing for the photographer, c. 1904.

A MEETING OF DOG LOVERS in the garden of the Vicarage at Congresbury, c. 1910.

STATION ROAD, Congresbury, *c.* 1900.

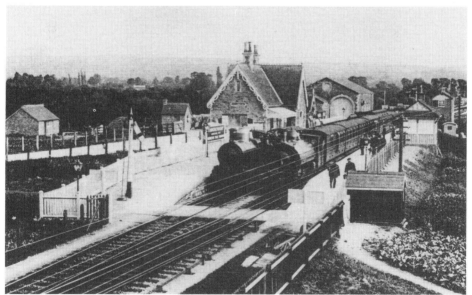

CONGRESBURY STATION, *c.* 1925, had been opened, with a single platform, on 3 August 1869, on the line from Yatton to Wells. In 1901 the second platform was added when the Wrington Vale Light Railway opened its line from here to Blagdon. The station was closed on 1 July 1964 (passenger services had ceased on 2 September 1963) and the station buildings were demolished on 2 October 1968. Ironically, the rubble was tipped into the adjoining swamp which had been created in 1869 when earth was removed from the same area to build the embankments of the road bridge over the railway.

BROAD STREET, Wrington, c. 1905. A charter to hold a weekly market here on Tuesdays was granted in Edward II's reign but the market had virtually ceased before the end of the eighteenth century, though an annual Fair was then still being held on 9 September. The building on the far left in the photograph above, the Bell Inn, has now been converted to a garage but with the portico remaining. In the view below, looking in the opposite direction, the main changes today are the conversion of the building on the left to a bank and the corner part of the Golden Lion to a shop (Amor's Stores).

CHARLES VINER'S BAKER'S SHOP and bread delivery van on the south-west corner of Broad Street, Wrington, c. 1906. Mr Viner, in addition to his trade as a baker, was also a corn and meal merchant and the manufacturer of Moss Rose self-raising flour, for which he won a gold medal in London in September 1899. His shop front has since been removed from the building which has been restored to its original dwelling house appearance.

MR FRANCIS GEORGE KING'S BUTCHER'S SHOP at Wrington, c. 1910.

JOHN LOCKE, the philosopher, was born in this cottage, adjoining the churchyard, on 29 August 1632. He died on 28 October 1704 and when the cottage was demolished in 1891 and its site incorporated into the churchyard a plaque was erected to record the location.

THE WESLEYAN CHAPEL, Wrington, c. 1912. This building is now the Burrington and Wrington Scout and Guide Headquarters. Mr Amor, who took this photograph, and many others of Wrington, had a drapery shop in Broad Street and a grocery shop (seen on the left) in High Street. Although this High Street building is no longer Amor's, the name is still current on the corner of High Street and Broad Street.

WRINGTON SCHOOL, C. 1912. Opened on 1 May 1857, the school cost about £1,500 to erect and accommodated 245 children.

WRINGTON STATION, C. 1906. With only a 30-year life as a passenger station (4 December 1901 to 14 September 1931), goods were handled here for a further 30 years until total closure on 10 June 1963.

BARLEY WOOD, Wrington. Hannah More, authoress, philanthropist and, with her four sisters, founder of many schools in the area, built this cottage where they all lived from 1800. They had previously lived nearby, in a cottage they had built at Cowslip Green. She died in Bristol in 1833, aged 89, and is buried with her sisters in Wrington churchyard. This photograph, c. 1912, shows the cottage after considerable extensions by succeeding owners.

A MEET OF THE CLIFTON FOOT HARRIERS at Cowslip Green, Wrington, 22 October 1910. The name of this pack dates from 1894, but derives from the Clifton Harriers who hunted over Durdham Down, Bristol, in 1840. When Clifton residents objected to their 6.00 a.m. meets, hunting was moved to country areas around Bristol. The Hunt moved to kennels beside The Railway Hotel, Yatton, in 1890, and then to premises at Wemberham just before the First World War.

A PAUSE FOR A CHAT IN SILVER STREET, Wrington, c. 1910. The railings, since replaced by a stone wall, bound the front garden of a small cottage tucked into the angle between the buildings on the left. The building on the extreme left, which has been considerably rebuilt, including the removal of the fine porch, is now a veterinary clinic.

AN OX ROAST, believed to have taken place in the Congresbury area in the 1920s.

REDHILL, a hamlet of Wrington, C. 1925. The A38 road climbs steeply and for a considerable distance at this point and was a problem for early motorists. In the 1920s the lightly-powered small cars of the day could often manage to climb the hill only in reverse (being a lower gear than first) and even then had to stop at each short level stretch to allow the radiator to cool. The photograph above, from near the top of the hill, shows the Mendip Hills in the background and in the lower picture the car is parked outside the post office, with Christ Church, consecrated in January 1844, on the skyline.

SECTION SIX

Along the Turnpike Road

CLEEVE, c. 1930. This small village extends for some distance along the A370 road and in this view the bus from Bristol has just passed the post office, Mr S. Gray's shop and The Old Inn, originally a house of c. 1625, on its way to Weston-super-Mare.

137

HOLY TRINITY CHURCH, Cleeve, c. 1900. This church was erected in pseudo-Norman style in 1840, three years before Cleeve was formed into a separate ecclesiastical parish from Yatton, and sits at a high point beside the sinuous road through this part of the village.

JOHN WAIR supervises his tea-gardens at Cleeve, c. 1906. Advertised as a Cyclists' Rest, this was a popular place to stop for a refreshing (non-alcoholic) drink at the half-way point on a trip between Bristol and Weston-super-Mare.

THE LORD NELSON INN at Cleeve, c. 1909. At this date it was owned by the Ashton Gate Brewery Co., becoming a Georges Brewery house in 1932 (see photograph on page 2). In 1936 the new owners erected a modern public house, with the same name, much further back from the roadside, and demolished this old building.

HARROWING AT CLEEVE COURT, 1908. Cleeve Court had been built c. 1820 and incorporated material from the neighbouring twelfth-century Court de Wyck which had fallen into ruin in the eighteenth century. It has recently been converted for use as a private nursing home.

WILLIAM EACOTT, the Cleeve blacksmith, c. 1934. Starting work at the age of 15, Mr Eacott was then still working every day at the age of 87, claiming to be the oldest working farrier in the country. He was at Cleeve for 60 years and had never missed a day's work in his life.

COMPARATIVE VIEWS OF THE MAIN ROAD AT CLEEVE, C. 1900 (above) and C. 1925 (below). Allowing for the fact that the earlier photograph was taken in winter and the later one in summer, there had been little change during the 25-year period. Comparison with the photograph on page 137 shows that there was a considerable change, however, in the following five years.

CLEEVE SCHOOL, c. 1935. The school building, on the right, had been erected in 1836 and enlarged in 1860 to accommodate 80 children. The house on the left is a c. 1600 building adapted (and probably re-roofed at the same time) for use as the Master's house when the school was built. The house has been much modernized including all external details.

JUBILEE DAY, 1935, at Cleeve. The scene outside the village school where the rising ground made an ideal grandstand to watch the events taking place.

TWO GROUPS OF CLEEVE SCHOOLCHILDREN. Above, in 1912, the boys are wearing very formal clothes, many with large stiff collars, while the girls' dress is much more varied and informal. Below, in 1928, both boys and girls wear more varied clothing though the girl on the left in the front row is wearing boots reminiscent of 30 years earlier.

ST NICHOLAS CHURCH AND BROCKLEY COURT, c. 1906. Brockley Court was the home of the Pigott and later Smyth-Pigott families and the building seen here was built by them at the end of the seventeenth century to replace the original Court building (now Brockley Court Farm). The church, of Norman origin, was extensively rebuilt between 1820 and 1830 at the expense of the Pigotts. Brockley Court is now used as a home for the elderly.

BROCKLEY COTTAGE, c. 1910. This delightful, secluded cottage was probably a former sixteenth-century farmhouse. A small building near the cottage is said to have been built to house an elephant imported by the East India Co., that was used for timber hauling in the woods.

BROCKLEY COMBE, on the opposite side of the A370 to the village. A 1900 winter scene in this beautiful gorge where the rock faces are mainly hidden by trees and bushes. It was a popular carriage drive for the Victorian ladies from Brockley Court and Brockley Hall.

WEST TOWN, Backwell, c. 1909. Two unattended horses enjoy some food from the wooden trough outside The New Inn while the carters are, no doubt, taking their refreshment inside. Almost opposite is the original building of The Rising Sun, demolished with two ancient, adjacent cottages in 1937 and replaced by the present building.

THE MAIN ROAD, West Town, Backwell, looking towards Bristol, c. 1906, at the junction with Church Lane.

A DENNIS TANKER LORRY and a group of workmen employed by Joseph Coles and Son, haulage and general contractors at West Town, Backwell, for many years from the 1920s.

A FARMHOUSE OR COTTAGE, believed to have been at West Town, Backwell, in the early 1900s. A positive identification by any reader of the building and/or the family standing outside would be welcomed.

HILLSIDE LANE, leading from the crossroads in the centre of present-day Backwell to Church Town, is little altered at its upper end from this c. 1909 view; even a thatched cottage still survives, near the church. The top stage of St Andrew's Church tower does not match the building style of the lower stages which were built c. 1428. It has been suggested that this is because it was rebuilt, following extensive damage during a storm in 1603 but this theory does not explain why one pinnacle is so different from the others.

BACKWELL SCHOOL, 1868. A W.R. Stock photograph taken six years after the school, with adjoining Master's house, was built and before the 1873 and 1892 enlargements. A recent prefabricated building provides further additional accommodation.

BACKWELL PARISH HALL, soon after its opening by the Marquess of Bath on 6 April 1910. Although the building has changed little in 80 years, the surroundings have altered considerably.

A SCOUT GROUP FROM BACKWELL has travelled to Bristol in the 1920s to deliver rabbits to the Vicar of St Lawrence Church, Lawrence Hill, for distribution to the poor of the district. The horse and cart belonged to Charles Owen, a Farleigh farmer.

THE RUINED ENGINE HOUSE of New Pit coalmine, Backwell, c. 1900. The buildings of Nailsea station can just be seen on the left. New Pit was a very late attempt to continue mining coal in the area. The shaft was not sunk until 1861 when an effort was made to reach a coal seam, abandoned when the shaft collapsed at the earlier Amberlands Pit, situated on the opposite side of Station Road. However, although a depth of 336 feet had been reached by 1864, water problems caused abandonment here as well.

THE BACKWELL, NAILSEA & DISTRICT AGRICULTURAL CO-OPERATIVE SOCIETY LTD. operated from this building in Backwell's main street as wholesale and retail corn and meal merchants. The building seen in this 1920s photograph still exists but is used in another capacity.

JAMES MANNING'S SHOP in West Town, Backwell, c. 1905. Mr Manning was also the village sub-postmaster and by the 1920s his widow had taken over both the shop and post office.

THE MAIN (A370) ROAD THROUGH FARLEIGH, Backwell, looking towards Bristol, c. 1905, with a considerable amount of horse-drawn traffic. As in the picture on page 146, an unattended horse makes use of the wooden food trough. Such troughs were to be found outside many public houses in the area in those days.

FARLEIGH, Backwell, c. 1905. This photograph, looking in the opposite direction to the lower one on page 151, shows The George Inn, on the right, and unusually tall telephone poles (also visible in the previous photograph) that were erected through this village.

Parties catered for. Beautiful Gardens. Marquee in field attached. Unlimited Accommodation. Popular Charges.

THE GEORGE INN, Farleigh, Backwell, c. 1914, formerly called The Farley Inn; the change of name having taken place soon after 1786. Mr Hek, the landlord, would have been well pleased to receive the charabanc passengers' custom while the drivers stayed with their vehicles. This would not be an appropriate place to park four coaches today!

BARROW GURNEY IN THE 1920s. The Parish Room, in the foreground, was built in 1901 and later accommodated the village post office.

BARROW COURT AND CHURCH, Barrow Gurney, c. 1895. Built c. 1545 on the site of a former house which had been converted from a thirteenth-century nunnery, c. 1538, the building is the result of considerable extension and reconstruction. Used as a teacher training college for many years, it is now a complex of individual residential units.

BARROW GURNEY SCHOOL. The photograph above shows the school, which had been built in 1863 for 64 children, as it was in 1905. Below, from a picture postcard, sent by the Headmaster John Lee to the Headmaster of the National School at Worle, postmarked on 25 September 1906, is the same scene after the building had been totally destroyed by fire. A replacement school, for 80 pupils, was built in 1909, Mr Lee continuing as Headmaster.

BARROW HOUSE, Barrow Gurney, pre-1850. This house was purchased by Bristol Water Works Co. in 1851 and demolished to provide the site for the first of three reservoirs which the company constructed at Barrow in the nineteenth century to provide a water supply to Bristol.

ST MICHAEL'S CHURCH, Flax Bourton, C. 1890. Founded C. 1140 with many late-fourteenth- and fifteenth-century additions, the church was restored and enlarged in 1881, at a cost of £1160. The churchyard was not enclosed until 1803 nor consecrated for burials until 24 October 1812.

THE UNION WORKHOUSE, Flax Bourton, c. 1900. Opened on 4 December 1838 for the Bedminster Union Board of Guardians of the Poor, it came under the control of the Long Ashton Union from 1899 to 1930, when responsibility for such institutions was transferred from the Guardians to local Councils. On 1 January 1931 the name was changed to Cambridge House. In 1960 the building became Farleigh Hospital.

FLAX BOURTON STATION, c. 1890, looking to the tunnel beneath the road junction at Cambridge Batch. Opened in 1860 with the title Bourton, and changed to Flax Bourton on 1 September 1888, this station was replaced by a new station 500 yards down the line on 2 March 1893.

A BAZAAR, MARKET AND SPORTS DAY at Castle House, Flax Bourton, c. 1924.

THIS GABLED FARMHOUSE (possibly Elizabethan) housed the post office at Flax Bourton for many years from c. 1895. George Hiatt was the farmer owner and sub-postmaster at the time of this c. 1905 picture and he was followed as sub-postmaster by Henry James Hiatt from c. 1910 to the late 1920s. Earlier, Flax Bourton had been important in the postal service as, from July 1817, the Post Receiving House here started sorting letters, brought by the Bristol to Churchill rider, for delivery on foot to Wraxall, Nailsea, Clevedon and Walton-in-Gordano. This change raised its status to a forward sorting office.

A 'ROYAL BLUE' COACH, owned by Elliot Bros., Bournemouth, waits outside the Jubilee Inn, Flax Bourton, c. 1932, while the passengers take refreshment.

FLAX BOURTON, C. 1905, looking towards Long Ashton with St Michael's Church in the background and a village water supply in the centre of the road in the foreground.

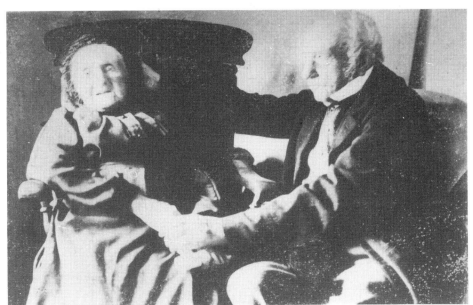

HONOR COLEMAN, aged 107, with the Chairman of the Long Ashton Union Board of Guardians, aged 88, at the Union Workhouse, Flax Bourton, 1907.

PROCLAMATION DAY, 1910, has been written on the back of the original photograph. The traction engine is drawing two wagons filled with children in their best clothes. Owners' names on the wagons are of Yatton firms and the building in the background carries Great Western Railway notice boards with posters advertising events at Weston-super-Mare, Bath and Bristol. This does not appear to be Yatton station, however, nor does the building seem to match any railway station within a day's traction engine drive from Yatton. Can any reader positively identify the location of this photograph please?

ACKNOWLEDGEMENTS

While most of the illustrations in this book are from original photographs in my private collection, a small number are from originals in the ownership of others and I extend my grateful thanks to those listed for their kind permission to reproduce photographs in their possession: Mrs R. Anstey, Mr J.G. Burgan, Mr P.G. Davey, Lt. Col. M. Flash, Mrs M. Harris, Mr R.W. Kidner, Mr W.F. Perry, Bristol Reference Library, Clevedon Library, Kingston Seymour Local History Society, Nailsea Library (Greenhill Donation) and Woodspring Museum.

I would also like to thank the following for their invaluable assistance in obtaining and providing factual information to enable me to compile a number of the captions: Marian Barraclough, Andy Brisley, Judith Codrington, Jane Evans, Cecil Knight, Bill Perry, Sharon Poole, Ken Stuckey, Margaret Thomas and Peter Wright.

As sources of verifying historic detail, I would like to acknowledge the use of publications produced by Congresbury History Group, Nailsea and District Local History Society, SCALA (Society for a Conservation Area in Long Ashton) and Yatton Local History Society.

I hope there are no errors in the captions, but if any reader has a correction to offer or can provide confirmation of uncertain facts I would welcome any advice, which can be forwarded through the publisher.